MW01138618

Let

"P. A. P. E. R."

Work for YOU!

A simple solution to keep

your skilled talent

from applicant to retirement!

Copyright © 2018 by Kenneth C. Lynch

ISBN # 978-0-578-21399-6
ISBN # 978-0-578-21485-6 (ebook)

All rights reserved.

Published in the United States of America by HR Diner, LLC

No part of this publication may be reproduced, distributed or transmitted in any form or by any means, including photocopying, recording or other electronic or mechanical methods, without the prior written permission of the publisher.

This book is dedicated to the
Professionals in Human Resources
for their dedication to servicing their
*customer: **the Employee**!*

Table of Contents

Let "P. A. P. E. R." *Work for You*!

Introduction

This book has been over 30 years in the making. The idea for this book originated while I was a 1st Lieutenant in the U. S. Army, stationed at Ft. Gillam, Georgia, back in 1986. During this time I discovered how much paperwork was involved in the military. However, within a brief span of time, I discovered paperwork was prevalent in most dealings within most government agencies as well. Upon leaving the military and entering the private sector, I discovered that it was not just a military or government phenomenon; paperwork was just a burdensome and prevalent in the civilian sector!

My career path took me into the field of Human Resources and I soon discovered how paperwork, when done correctly, would positively impact the most critical asset for success: the people working there – the employees....and in so doing, achieve the goals and objectives of the organization.

I have now been working in the field of Human Resources (HR), in one way or another, for almost 40 years! I have been a trainer, recruiter, personnel records specialist, department manager, mentor, coach and negotiator, just to name a few roles. These roles have exposed me to almost all aspects of HR such as records management, talent management, compensation and benefits, employee and labor relations, government compliance, change management, risk and safety, employee morale and engagement, and training and development. Additionally, these roles were strategic, tactical and operational in nature depending upon the urgency, the staffing within the HR Depart or the resources available. However, no matter what role I was in, my main focus was always on "my customer": the employee – the organization's greatest asset.

Throughout the years, how we (defined as employers) have treated our employees, as well as the influence of government rules and regulations, has dramatically changed. When I first started, we did not have to worry about government legislation like The Americans with Disabilities Act (ADA) or The Family Medical Leave Act (FMLA) because they did not exist. Sure there were guidelines, but they were more informal and not as stringent as they are today.

Of course, there were government agencies or regulations that did directly impact employees, such as the Equal Employment Opportunity Commission (EEOC), Fair Labor Standard Act (FLSA), Office of Federal Contract Compliance Programs (OFCCP) with Affirmative Action (AA), the National Labor Relations Board (NLRB) and Occupational Safety and Health Administration (OSHA). However, they were not as invasive (I know this word sounds negative, but I do not mean it to be!) as they are today because technology has greatly improved the government agencies' ability to regulate compliance and ensure employers are doing what is right for the employees.

Then, of course, we cannot discount how the political parties have influenced the workplace by creating new laws by the Legislative branch, executive orders by the Executive branch or interpretation of said laws and orders by the Judicial branch (both at the federal and state level). It is no wonder HR professionals have to continuously attend conferences and seminars to remain current on laws and regulations. If they did not stay current, then they would be putting their organizations at risk of not being compliant.

There is also another influence which brought me to writing this book. That is as an educator. I have been an Adjunct Professor at several global universities for the past 18 years, teaching mostly graduate level HR courses, which included 10 years teaching a certification course for HR professionals. I find teaching affords me the opportunity to not only share what knowledge I have, but to learn from the students who bring their experiences to the classroom. However, what my teaching experience has shown me is many younger HR professionals have not experienced the same HR-related issues and challenges that I have and yet, they are held accountable at their places of employment to "know" the answers. While this is not totally fair to the young HR professional, regrettably, that is the way it is.

My students hear me state these comments often about being in the HR field: "The longer you are in HR, the better you will be. I cannot teach you everything from a book. HR is one of the best occupations where on-the-job (OJT) training is the best way to learn." So though this book, I will be able to share some experiences and insight on HR that may be of benefit to the HR professional who has not had the same exposure as I have.

As I have mentioned, the employee is the most important asset an organization has. No matter how big or how small the organization, it takes an employee to create the product or provide the service the consumer needs. And as the organization grows and the size of the workforce grows, taking care of the employee becomes even more complicated. The organization becomes more "employee-focused" and creates a culture that tries to recruit and retain high performing employee. This creates the need for a trained and skilled manager to be in place to manage the workforce, supported by the HR Professional.

HR departments are lean. Luckily, the HR professional has many tools available to help manage the workforce. Unfortunately, while some of these tools are proven, some are not. Many are costly. Most are not developed "in house" or managed within the organization but by a third party. And many are too complex and too convoluted to manage with a small, lean HR department. So the HR professional is left to determine which tool(s) to use, to spend limited financial resources on and to commit his/her limited workhours to make things happen.

So why read this book? This book will assist the reader in dealing with that most important asset in the organization: the employee. It is written for the young HR professional just entering the HR field, as well as the seasoned HR professional who may be experiencing challenges with maintaining a productive and engaged workforce. This book presents ideas and suggestions which support strategic human talent management, as well as the day-to-day operational interactions between supervisors and employees. The objective of the book is to present a simple solution, maybe even a "silver bullet" so to speak, to keep the key players in your organization all the way from the applicant phase to retirement. And by following this simple solution, you just might be able to retain the engaged, loyal and productive employees your organization requires and deserves.

(NOTE: Websites referenced in this book may change or no longer be accessible. The publisher of this book is not responsible for those sites or their content.)

Chapter 1

"In the beginning…."

The Holy Bible states, "In the beginning God created the sky and the earth, then light, then the oceans and land, then the animals and everything living, then finally, human beings." (Genesis, Chapter 1).

In the world of Human Resources, in the beginning, there is the applicant. Who is this applicant you ask? The applicant is your future employee – the one who becomes the active employee, who will create the product or the service to sell, who will establish the relationship with the customer, who will make the delivery, who will perform the "after the sale" service, who will manage other employees, who will constantly think of new ways to do things to stay competitive in the market, who will work with other employees in a collaborate manner to make sure the organization survives and who, at the end of the day, will take home a paycheck so he/she and his/her family can do what they want to do. The applicant is the lifeblood and the future of the organization. In a nutshell, the applicant IS the organization!

Unfortunately, the applicant, the "right" applicant, does not just appear. Someone has to find the "right" applicant. So, who is responsible for looking for the applicant? Who has the responsibility to see if the applicant has the skills the organization needs and will fit into the culture of the organization, to ensure the "right" applicant becomes an employee, to make sure the new employee is taken care of throughout his/her employment relationship with the organization? The answer: the Human Resources (HR) professional.

It is the responsibility of HR to not only know how to recruit the right applicants for the organization, but to make sure the organization fulfills its legal obligations as prescribed under the laws, rules and regulations of the government, as well as the policies and procedures of the organization, once the applicant becomes an employee.

To accomplish this task, HR must be current on what the government requires at the federal, state and local levels. HR must be cognizant of the environmental factors surrounding the talent management process (this includes recruiting, retention, training and professional development). HR must understand the psychology of people, of leadership and of motivation. HR must be involved in the development of viable compensation and benefit programs that satisfy the intrinsic and extrinsic rewards sought after by the employees. HR must do what it takes to keep the "right" applicant in the organization for as long as the "right" applicant – now the "right" employee – contributes to the success of the organization. This is a daunting task for a department that is normally understaffed and where the HR professional performs multiple tasks under the title of "HR Generalist".

There is a rule of thumb about how many HR professionals should be in the HR Department. Years ago, it was one HR professional for every 100 employees. Then it became one for every 150 employees. Today, it is roughly one for every 200 to 250 employees. Of course, if your organization is large enough to be able to centralize specific HR functions (for example:

recruiting, compensation & benefits, risk & safety, leave administration or training and development) into sub-departments of the HR department, then you can enlarge the HR department staff. Or, if you cannot grow your HR department, maybe your organization can farm out these processes to a third party vendor so your existing HR staff can focus on the critical HR functions that strategically make your organization competitive in the war for recruiting and retaining skilled talent.

I would be remiss if I didn't make a quick comment about the one key contributor to the streamlining of HR departments: technology! As more and more HR functions became automated and farmed out, there was less and less of a need for a "human" to perform those functions. Thus, organizations either found new duties for its HR staff or downsized. On the positive side, though, by automating or outsourcing many of the day-to-day functions, this allowed HR professionals to become more strategic minded and allowed to have a great impact on the organization. (Personal note: I don't know about you, but I sure was happy when outside vendors provided software programs to manage the Affirmative Action Program and EEO 1 reporting. These types of activities were a pain to perform manually!!!)

It is important to note that most companies are not the mega corporations we see on the Fortune lists (50, 100, 500, 1,000, etc.). Instead, most companies are smaller, "Mom and Pop" businesses, with the in-house HR duties being performed by someone who is in a non-HR role/department and as an additional duty. This pseudo-HR professional is more involved in the day-to-day personnel duties than the wide range of HR functions that a trained HR professional may perform.

Thankfully over the past 30 years or so, we have seen where organizations have begun to realize that having a trained HR professional on staff not only helps with the recruiting and retention efforts, but also helps minimize the legal risks associated with wrongful hires, discharges and violating government compliance guidelines. By minimizing the legal risks, this helps build positive and creative culture within the organization.

We have also seen over the years, colleges and universities offering undergraduate and graduate degrees in HR and HR-related fields. HR professional associations emerged. Training organizations, focused on the HR profession, developed and offered certification courses to aid in the standardization of the skills HR professionals should have, depending upon their role within the organization (operational, strategic, tactical or global level).

Today, we find the experienced, trained HR professional is a degreed individual, possessing at least one HR professional certification, who is engaged in a battle – against other HR professionals, I might add – in the war to recruit and retain skilled talent. The HR professional has to find new ways to locate workers, convince the workers to join their organization and most importantly, find ways to satisfy the needs of the workers so they will STAY at the organization. And that is where this book comes into play.

Chapter 2

"Today...Tomorrow...But Don't Go Too Far Out..."

At the time this book was written, the economic and social environment in the United States was (and probably still is) in a state of confusion. Political parties were fighting with each other, as well as within the party itself. Congress was not working well with the White House and vise versa. There was confusion over tax reform and healthcare reform. Global tensions were on the rise. Interest rates were going up. There were many questions with very few clear answers. But regardless of who did what, or maybe we should say who did NOT do anything when they could have done something, at the end of the day, organizations still needed to operate. Organizations still needed to be functioning, be profitable and take care of its stakeholders: the employees, the community, the vendors and suppliers, and the customers!

It seems pretty simple to me why we (local communities and its citizens, private and public companies, and government agencies) would want the economic environment to be healthy. Think of a circle. An organization hires people. People make and deliver the goods and services the organization sells. The organization provides its employees benefits and wages. These employees go out and spend their wages in the community. The community thrives. More people move into the thriving community. More goods and services are needed in the community to satisfy the demands of the growing community. The organization hires more employees to satisfy that demand of the community. Oh, and do not forget the organization, as well as the employees, pay taxes that help run the programs needed in the community and for the government services provided to the community. And guess who is smack dab in the middle of this circle? The HR professional!

As the HR professional, we need to look at the environment we are in today. We need to do this quick analysis before we can focus on our employees. We need to look at the economy. We need to look at the labor force availability. We need to look at who is running the government. We need to look at what is going on around the world. Even if the HR professional works in a small "Mom and Pop" that doesn't expand its reach outside the city limits, the HR professional must be proactive and aware of what can impact the company not only today, but also tomorrow and beyond.

Let us do a quick look at the economy. The economy is strong and growing between 2.5% and 3%. Unemployment is at a level not seen in decades. The stock markets have hit record highs. Wages are rising, but slowly. Organizations are hiring. Globalization is commonplace. Sounds great….right? Wrong….do not get too excited because with globalization also comes the challenges associated with countries who have different philosophies (government practices, economic policies, trade agreements, taxes, tariffs, etc….) and these differences could negatively impact our own economy at any time. But I digress…let us get back to our associates – both current and future.

It is almost the end of 2018 and the federal unemployment rate is still below 4.0%. This is exciting news because many economists believe an unemployment rate under 5% is basically full employment in our economy. (Keep in mind, if you examine the U6 measurement, unemployment is more around 7% to 8%.) But while on the surface this is a positive reflection on our economy, it presents employers (meaning HR professionals who have to recruit and retain qualified employees) with many challenges.

The first major challenge is finding and recruiting the skilled talent necessary to do the day-to-day operations in the organization. With almost full employment, locating the skilled talent in your marketplace may be your biggest challenge. Sometimes, you might have to go outside your labor market and start recruiting from other labor markets; thus, incurring relocation costs and possibly paying higher than normal wages. We already do this for the more key or senior positions in the organization. However, if your local labor market is too tight or lacking of skilled talent even at the lower levels, you may have to open up your recruiting net to other markets and cities where there is skilled labor.

A second major challenge deals with training costs. Even when you find skilled labor to hire, you still need to train the new hire on your own proprietary systems, procedures and processes. But you may have to compound the training expense several times if you have to hire an untrained/unskilled worker and then train on site (commonly called "on-the-job" training) from the very beginning. To be sure, training is costly: cost of the training itself (materials, the training facility, maybe travel to/from the training...oh, and do not forget the salary of the trainer), as well as the lost productivity while the employee is in training, during the learning curve after the training and up to when the employee is fully trained and contributing back to the company. This contribution is called the return on the investment (ROI) of training.

A third challenge will be retaining your skilled labor. With such low unemployment and the shortage of skilled labor, organizations are scampering looking for skilled talent. Unfortunately, those organizations, in particular your competition, will be trying to steal away YOUR skilled talent! So how do you keep your employees? What retention initiatives do you have in place that will keep your employees loyal to your organization? Will you have to modify your compensation structure, meaning pay more, so you do not "lag" in the battle of wages?

The last challenge I want to address focuses on the culture of your organization. Do you know what your culture is? Have you identified your culture? Does everyone in the organization know what your culture is? Can your employees describe your culture? Is it the same description? Do others in the community know about your culture? More importantly, does your company have the culture that potential employees look for? Are you an "employer of choice"? This challenge is critical in not only recruiting great talent, but is critical in retaining that great talent!

So as you can see, there are some serious challenges we, in HR, have to experience when it comes to staffing our organizations. And unfortunately, many of the external factors (politics, global events, availability of skilled labor, etc.) that influence our staffing efforts are out of our control. But we can control the internal factors (recruiting, training, retention and culture) that influence our ability to recruit and retain the skilled talent necessary to sustain and grow our organizations!

Chapter 3

"Diversity Defines Who We Are"

There has been a lot, and I mean a lot, of material written about diversity and the value it brings to an organization. Starting with the theories presented in the classroom, followed by the research conducted in the field and ending with the financial results organizations post, diversity initiatives have been proven to positively impact the bottom line.

So, what is diversity? Even the definition of diversity is diverse! You will be hard pressed to find a definition that is universally agreed upon within academia and practitioners in the workplace because questions persist. Every organization is different and has to answer its own questions. For example, what constitutes our diverse organization? What factors influence the diversity composition within our organization?

In order to answer some of these questions, we need to establish a foundation of common concepts to agree upon.

Webster's dictionary defines diversity as this: "*the condition of having or being composed of different elements; the inclusion of different types of people (such as people of different races or cultures) in a group or organization*."

R. Roosevelt Thomas, Jr., a leading expert on diversity management, wrote that "*diversity refers to any mixture of items characterized by difference and similarities*."

Herman Melville, who penned the book Moby-Dick over a hundred and fifty years ago, wrote "*You cannot spill a drop of American blood without spilling the blood of the whole world.*" What I propose is this simple definition: "the very first time you and I differ – in anything, then diversity exists." This difference can be in any physical characteristic or mental thought. Remember what they say in the police dramas on TV, "there are no two sets of finger prints alike." If that is the case, then there are no two people alike; thus, everyone is different in one way or another from everyone else. Therefore, diversity exists whenever two or more people come together.

Now that we understand what diversity is, how does diversity impact the HR practitioner? We can start with how HR looks at the human assets (the employees) within the organization. By this I mean when HR looks at employees, HR looks at what knowledge, skills and abilities (KSAs) the employees bring to the organization. The greater the KSAs the employees have the greater value they bring to the organization. This value is what the organization uses to differentiate itself from its competition. This is the organization's human capital – its business value. But I think it is safe to say that some employees do not have the same levels of KSAs when compared to other employees. Thus, utilizing my definition of diversity here, it is easy to state the workplace is organically a diverse environment.

I want to introduce another concept that impacts diversity. It comes from the theory that you are a product of not only your environment, but what you bring since birth. Take a look at this wheel.

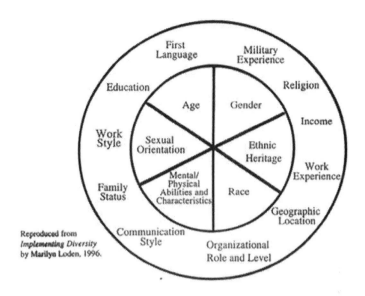

Reproduced from *Implementing Diversity* by Marilyn Loden, 1996.

This wheel is called the Dimensions of Workforce Diversity. I affectionately call the wheel the "forces of influence" because it breaks down all the key areas that made, and continue to make, us who we are today. It also demonstrates how we are all different because it is impossible for us to be impacted and respond in the same way by all of these influences.

As you look at the wheel, you will see that the inside wheel is made up influences we really can't change or are out of our control. This is what you bring since birth. For example, I can't be any younger than I am at this moment because time never stands still. I was born physically intact, so I was not born with a disability (even though I may develop one later in life). And, thanks to all the work my Grandmother did on our genealogy, I know where my family originated from.

The outside wheel shows the influences we have more control over. For example, I served 12 years in the U. S. Army, attend church with my family, have been working at least two jobs for the past 21 years and am finishing up a Doctorate degree to complete my formal education. So as you can see, I had the ability to influence in some manner the influences on the outer ring. They influenced me as I grew up and continue to have an influence on my behavior and personality – both at home and at work – as I grow older.

Now, when you combine the Dimensions of Workforce Diversity with the employee's KSAs, you will see how totally diverse our workforce is and why it may be difficult to work with others in the workplace. HR professionals, in particular, must be diligent and proactive in leading the diversity initiatives within the organization. And while HR incorporates diversity initiatives in the workplace, HR must also encourage and gain the support of upper management to support the diversity initiatives. Successful diversity cultures are championed from senior leadership down to the mail room clerk.

But there is more to diversity…..we cannot forget the differences in generations that are present in the workplace!

Chapter 4

"Another Generation Hits The Workplace!"

In today's work environment, it is quite possible you will be working alongside people who are younger than you, your same age and older than you. We tend to categorize people into the generation in which they come from. And as we discovered in the last chapter, since everyone is different, this adds some unique generational diversity to the work environment. So to get a better grasp of worker personalities and possibly how to influence workers to be more productive at work, we need to look at the different generations that are present in the workplace.

I think it is safe to say there are up to five (5) different generations found in the workplace today:

1. Traditionalists (Silent): born between 1925 - 1945
2. Baby Boomers (Boomers): born between 1946 - 1964
3. Generation X (Gen X): born between 1965 - 1980
4. Generation Y (Gen Y): born between 1981 - 2000
5. Generation Z (Gen Z): born after 2000

[Note: many like to combine Gen Y and Gen Z together and call this group the Millennials, even though Gen Z is starting to display its own unique characteristics from Gen Y. For this book, I will combine both Gen Y and Gen Z into one and refer to them collectively as Millennials.]

Before I try to explain the differences of each generation, I need to make this disclaimer. My comments are generalizations and yes, may sound like I am stereotyping those individuals within a specific generation. But as explained by the "forces of influence wheel", folks within the same generation may have been influenced by the same environmental forces; thus, they may display the same behaviors. In any event, in HR we try to help determine behavioral patterns and understand the differences in generations.

Okay, let us look at each generation in a little more detail.

The Traditionalists were born before and up to the end of World War II. Traditionalists experienced the Great Depression, food lines, unemployment then war: World War II and Korea. They were the first to use the telephone, watch television and saw dramatic advancements in medicine. Families were traditional with a father and mother, married and living close to where the grandparents were. The men went to technical school or college and the women were stay-home caregivers. But one thing we saw in the business world during World War II was the introduction of women in the workplace in large numbers. These women occupied the work roles that the men wore filling prior to the war; only to be removed when the war ended and the men returned. It was common for a Traditionalist to work for one employer in an entire lifetime. Their work culture was to do as they were told, without asking any questions as to why they were doing what they were asked to do.

The Boomers, like the previous generation, had a similar work culture: do as told and do not ask why. They might have work for just one employer throughout their career, but it was not uncommon for a Boomer to work for 3 – 5 different employers in a career. Employers still treated employees as a means to an end and did not really take the time to understand the employees or what their needs were. Dads still worked outside the home while Moms still stayed home. During this generation, Boomers experienced the Cold War and the threat of the A-bomb, economic growth and the introduction of quality control at work, the Viet Nam War (also known as the "Unpopular War"), the civil rights movement, feminism, presidents being shot at and one being assassinated, color TV, movies at the theater that dealt with the realities - both good and bad - of society and space travel. The work ethic of a Boomer was still to be loyal to the employer, follow the rules, avoid conflict and try to politically move up the corporate ladder.

Gen Xers introduced a new employee: one who was more independent, open-minded, and confident, liked a fast-paced environment and challenged the status quo. But unlike the Traditionalist and Boomer who lived so they could go to work, the Gen X worker worked so they could live his/her life and pursue his/her own personal interests. This change forced employers to change how they valued the employee because the employee was now changing jobs about 11 – 15 times in a career. The events that influenced this generation are the end of the Cold War, the first Desert Storm, personal computers, cellular phones, MTV, divorce, the energy crisis and more and more working Mothers.

[Note: I do not know if it just me, but for the past few years, it seems all the published articles about the different generations only focused on the Boomers and Millennials. What about the

Gen Xers? Why was there nothing written about them? Maybe we should start calling the Gen Xers the "Lost Generation"!!!]

Today, the HR focus seems to concentrate solely on the newest generation: the Millennials. The Millennials are a digital generation that is very optimistic, focused on civic duty and social consciousness, confident in their actions, have a respect for diversity, achievement oriented and are tenacious in working towards their goals. Employers are now modifying their work cultures for this generation as this generation is becoming the largest segment of the workforce. Millennials want feedback on their performance, like to multitask, must have access to the Internet and social media, like short and to the point messages and direction, like to be challenged, enjoy having a mentor and use collaboration and team building to help find solutions.

Now, before I end this quick introduction to the different generations, I want to share some insights into the newest Millennial generation: Gen Z. This generation is totally digital and social media focused; they have never been without just-in-time communication and access to the Internet. Additionally, they have a global mindset, with local reality, and are totally immersed in diversity. Unfortunately, the drawbacks to this digital generation are the shortfall in interpersonal communication and relationships, lack of non-technical skills and undeveloped critical thinking skills. Oh, and they are entering the workforce for the first time.

One final thought. Be careful about using labels when talking to a multi-generational workforce. These labels are, again, just common characteristics of very large populations.

What you need to remember is these characteristics may not be common to your workplace. Your workplace may be different because of your geographic location, composition of your workforce (think race, color, creed, national origin, gender, age, Veteran status, disability status, pregnancy status, sexual orientation), industry (profit versus non-profit; public, private or government), tenure of your workers, etc.

Let me share a quick story. I was speaking at a conference in Portland recently and one of the attendees stated he was a Boomer and in his viewpoint, the Millennials were "lazy with a poor work ethic". Then a couple other Boomers said the same thing, as did some Gen Xers. I immediately looked at the Millennials in the room and saw, in their body language, that they were becoming upset. The Millennials, obviously, took offence at those statements. And when I asked one of the Millennials if she was upset over the Boomer's statement, she said she was and in fact, was quite the opposite: she described herself as a "workaholic", totally dedicated to her profession. She felt she worked just as hard and was just as dedicated at the Boomer was.

So, again, be very careful when making generalizations about people. Remember, we are all different. We all have different experiences, motivations, goals and dreams. (Refer to the forces of influence as discussed in the previous chapter.) Be careful because there are so many variables that contribute to the makeup of our individual workers and the workforce as a whole, as well as the culture of the organization.

Chapter 5

A Quick Look at Motivation and Leadership Styles

I always say it is difficult to have good interpersonal relationships between yourself and fellow co-workers unless you know "who you are" first. This is especially true if you are a manager or supervisor. So in this chapter, I want to present some fundamental motivational factors and leadership styles for you to think about. I will keep the discussion on motivation and leadership styles at a "high level", as to avoid getting to deep into my academia background. However, I highly recommend to the reader to dive deeper into these two areas if your knowledge is limited because these two areas are critical in the foundation of solid interpersonal relationships at work. Just keep in mind the key principal to remember is this: WE ARE ALL DIFFERENT!!!!

Motivation

There are two types of motivation: intrinsic motivation and extrinsic motivation. When I present these two types of motivation in training seminars, I like to present the two types like this: intrinsic is what motivates from inside your brain and extrinsic is what motivates from outside your brain. Let us look at these two in greater detail.

Intrinsic motivation is where a person performs activities or actions that will make the person feel good on the inside. These actions have some importance to the person by satisfying a need or supporting a belief; the greater the importance, the higher the motivation. Some examples of intrinsic motivation

19

are acceptance (where others feel good about your actions or decisions), honor (the feeling you get when you follow the rules or are ethical when others are not), power (the feeling you get when you can influence others), or social status (the feeling you get when others think you are important).

Extrinsic motivation is where a person feels good because of outside stimuli. For example, as an employee, you are motivated to get up in the morning and go to work because you need a paycheck; thus, money would be the motivator. (NOTE: How much a person's motivation is derived from money is usually a topic of debate in the HR community because not everyone is motivated in the same way by money alone.) Other examples of extrinsic motivators are awards, bonuses, promotions, paid training or professional development courses. It should be noted that while these stimuli are from the outside environment and not inside the brain, many times a person receives extrinsic motivators that also stimulate the brain and create intrinsic motivation, thus heightening the total motivational experience.

Now that we know the two types of motivation, the next step would be to see how motivation impacts the workplace. Since the early 1900's, motivation has been studied extensively to see how it impacts the workplace, in particular employee productivity. There are numerous theories on employee motivation; however, I find myself always leaning towards three main motivational theories. These three are commonly taught in management professional development courses and may sound familiar to you. They are Abraham Maslow's "Hierarchy of Needs", Frederick Hertzberg's "Two-Factor Theory" and Victor Vroom's "Expectancy Theory".

The first theory, the Hierarchy of Needs, is more commonly known as Maslow's Pyramid and has identified five basic needs: physiological (the most basic: food, shelter, water), safety (personal and financial security, good health), belongingness (friendships, relationships, family), esteem (be confident and respected by others) and self-actualization (the highest need: achieving everything you possibly can). Per Maslow, a person starts with the most basic need (physiological) and can only progress [up the pyramid] to the next higher need AFTER the need below has been satisfied. Additionally, Maslow theorized that a person rarely reaches self-actualization because few, if any, of us ever truly achieves everything possible in our lives.

The second theory, the Two Factor Theory, is more commonly known as Hertzberg's Motivation-Hygiene Theory. Hertzberg believed there were two factors that influence motivation and satisfaction: motivation factors and hygiene factors. Motivation factors impact employee satisfaction in a positive manner and motivates the employee to work harder. Examples would be being recognized for a job well done, promotion or even just enjoying your job on a daily basis. Hygiene factors, when absent, causes employee dissatisfaction and demotivates an employee. For example, lack of an adequate salary or good benefits, poor company policies, or bad relationships with managers and co-workers.

If you try to compare Hertzberg's Two-Factor theory to Maslow's Hierarchy of Needs Theory, you may see Hertzberg's hygiene factors are similar to Maslow's physiological, safety and belongingness needs; whereas Hertzberg's motivational factors are similar to Maslow's esteem and self-actualization needs.

The third motivational theory is the Expectancy Theory. Vroom believed a person will behave or act a certain way because the person expects a specific result will occur. Basically, a person's motivation is based upon how that person desires the expected outcome. However, Vroom also felt that the person must cognitively process potential actions or behaviors first, before the final action or behavior is selected. So, this theory is based upon a mental process of choosing.

There are three elements within the Expectancy Theory: Expectancy, Instrumentality and Valence. Expectancy is what you believe the results will be from your action or behavior and is based upon prior experiences, self-confidence or the difficulty in the goal. Instrumentality is the belief that you will receive a reward if you meet your expectations. Valance is the value you place upon the reward.

So, which theory if best? Which one should you use? The correct answer: Use them all!!!

I like to think of motivation this way: if an employee's basic (paycheck, safety at work, good relationships with co-workers and supervisors) and higher (rewarding work environment and the chance to do/be recognized for doing something above and beyond the normal duties of the job description) needs are satisfied, plus the rewards of doing a good job are of value to the employee, then the employee will be motivated to come to work as scheduled, on time, and be productive. But if one or more of these motivators are not satisfied, then you, as a manager, must find a way to satisfy that need for the employee.

I know I make this sound easy to do and, in reality, many times it becomes very difficult to accomplish. However, the key here is you must try and find out what makes your employees "tick"…what motivates them to come to work and be productive. And when done properly, productivity and retention increase!

Leadership Styles

Depending upon the research you review, you will discover there are multiple types of leadership styles. Also in your research, you may stumble upon discussions on whether good leaders are "born" that way or are "developed" into good leaders. Thankfully, I am going to avoid that debate because over my 40 years in the workplace, both civilian and military, I have my own opinions on successful leaders; regrettably, I do not have the research/proof to support my opinions. But I will share that I believe good leaders know how to accommodate and modify their natural leadership style to fit the environment, the people they are dealing with or the situation at hand. (This is commonly referred to as eclectic leadership.) Successful leaders have learned to adjust themselves and not force others to adjust.

Leadership style research has identified 10 definable leadership styles. Some of these styles will seem very easy to understand, while some may be a little more difficult to grasp. Below are the 10 styles and a real-life example of a leader who displays that leadership style.

1. Autocratic (Authoritarian) Leadership: the leader has total authority and exhorts complete power over

everyone. Example: Kim Jong-un, Supreme Leader of North Korea.

2. Bureaucratic Leadership: the leader uses rules and procedures, as established by higher authority, to manage and make decisions. (Think about how we always say there is so much "red tape" in our government.) Example: Winston Churchill, Prime Minister of the United Kingdom during World War II.

3. Charismatic Leadership: the leader has a self-image so strong, people are naturally drawn to the leader. Example: John F. Kennedy, 35th President of the United States. However, one needs to be careful because people will follow charismatic leaders even if they do not totally agree with the viewpoints of the leader. It is like the people are blinded by the charisma and will follow blindly. Example: Adolf Hitler in his early years as a member of the National Socialist German Workers' Party.

4. Laissez-Faire Leadership: the leader has earned the trust of the people and delegates down to the people, only getting involved when necessary. Example: Mahatma Gandhi, activist who used non-violent, civil disobedience in India's journey to independence.

5. Participative (Democratic) Leadership: the leader listens and uses the opinions of the people by engaging them during the decision-making process. Example: Indra Nooyi, Chairwoman and CEO of PepsiCo.

6. Relationship-oriented Leadership: the leader inspires and motivates the people to achieve the goals of the organization by focusing on interacting with the people. Example: John Wooden, men's basketball Head Coach at UCLA from 1945 to 1975.

7. Servant Leadership: the leader leads by example, putting the people first – treating everyone equally. Example: Mother Teresa, founder of the Missionaries of Charity.

8. Transformational Leadership: the leader uses empathy and a good working relationship with the people to get them engaged. The Transformational leader "walks the talk" so the people will want to be the best they can be. This leadership style is viewed as the best style to have in the business environment. Example: Steve Jobs, co-founder of Apple.

9. Task-oriented Leadership: the leader sets deadlines and works with the people to get the tasks done by the deadline. There is a strong focus on proficiency and achieving goals. This leadership style is probably the most commonly used in the business environment. Example: Vladimir Lenin, leader of the Soviet Russia/Union from 1917 to 1924.

10. Transactional (Managerial) Leadership: the leader sets standards, supervises, evaluates and rewards/disciplines the people who work for the leader. Example: Bill Gates, co-founder of Microsoft.

I have noticed in the workplace two common leadership actions that many managers display when working on projects. The first one is where the manager just "tells" their employees what to do and leaves them alone. While this may sound great for the professional development of the subordinates, without guidance and the proper resources, the manager may be setting the subordinates up for failure....and unfortunately, many organizations are not very forgiving when employees fail. This failure is reflected in poor performance reviews, lower pay increases or even worse, termination.

Employee-centric and progressive organizations, such as high tech organizations, promote a "trial and error" culture and are forgiving, even supportive, when employees take a risk and fail. Think about Thomas Edison and his pursuit of the lightbulb. Mr. Edison stated, "I have not failed. I've just found 10,000 ways that it won't work." What he was saying was Instead of repeating the same mistakes, he learned from each mistake and made improvements until he was successful.

The second common leadership action is to just do the task at hand himself/herself, because it is easier to just do the task then spend a lot of time and energy to get the employees to do it correctly. But when you think about that statement, is that what the manager is paid to do – to do the work of the others? Or is the manager being paid to lead others to do the work they were hired to do, even if they do not really like the work they are being asked to do? Plus, when the manager does the work, this prevents the subordinates from learning and growing professionally...in subsequently, prevents them from becoming available for further responsibility and even promotions.

Now there is a twist to the manager doing the work for the subordinates. The twist is when the subordinates get the manager to do the work without the manager even knowing he/she is doing it. Let me give you an example of a terrific training event. It is called the "monkey on the back" scenario.

The scenario starts off with the manager giving each of the five subordinates a task (a task is a "monkey") and saying, "if you need help, just come see me." Well, needless to say, one by one, each subordinate kept coming to the manager, saying help was needed, and each time the manager said, "okay, let me see what I can do to get you help/the issue resolved." (Now picture the manager at his/her desk and each time the subordinate gets his/her manager to help, the subordinate places a "monkey" on the manager's back.) The more the manager helped, the longer the task ("monkey") stayed with the manager. Over time, as the manager was performing more and more subtasks for each subordinate, which, by the way, took the manager away from his/her own duties, the subordinates were allowed to avoid working on their assigned task. In the end, the manager ended up doing most of the work on each task (and had five "monkeys" on his/her back!) for the subordinates. So who was delegating to whom????

Oh….one more thing. This discussion would not be complete without a quick look at Emotional Intelligence (EI), first introduced by Michael Beldoch in 1964. EI is the ability to know your own emotions and recognize the emotions of your people, then use that emotional information to help guide/manage others to adapt to ever-changing situations or achieve specific goals. I only bring up EI because there are so many papers and articles out there that say EI is critical for successful leadership. Unfortunately, for every paper that supports EI, there seems to be another paper that cannot find any definitive correlation between EI and successful leadership. However, I think since EI deals with recognizing emotions, both in the leader and the people the leader is dealing with, is critical in positive interpersonal relationships. Thus, having a strong EI level may be a trait found in successful leaders.

So what is YOUR leadership style? Think about how you act as a leader. What is your strongest trait? Which of these leadership styles do you tend to use most often? Do you mix different styles to fit the situation? Do you use empathy when dealing with others? Do you take the time to learn what motivates the people you work with and try and use the proper motivators?

It is important you know who you are because I believe if you are able to modify and adjust your leadership style, when you are dealing with the people (individually) you work with, you will be more successful in getting the people to perform to expectations, and, in return, they will feel good about their performance too!!! This will make you a more successful leader.

Chapter 6

What Does the Labor Market Look Like Today?

The labor market, as well as the US economy as a whole, has undergone tremendous change in the past 12 years. Relax....I am not going to turn this chapter into an economics discussion or try to explain why there was a US recession (which went global) that lasted from 2008 to 2010, even though some experts believe the hangover of the recession lasted until 2012. However, it is necessary to understand the past so that if negative events do occur again in the future, you will be ready to respond.

In the business world, organizations must be focused on the future and meeting its future goals and objectives. To accomplish this, organizations must focus on the critical, number one asset required to meet those goals and objectives: skilled talent - otherwise known as employees who are trained to do the job!!!! Therefore, it is imperative for HR, in particular the recruiters of the organization, to know what talent currently exists within the organization, what skills are still needed, where to find the qualified talent and how to recruit and retain this skilled talent.

(Disclaimer: for this book, I am using the most current labor market information available from the Bureau of Labor and Statistics (BLS: www.bls.gov) and the Department of Labor (DOL: www.dol.gov) websites, as well as articles published by economists and financial institutions. So, if the information is wrong, do not blame me!)

Looking at the labor market, the first number that most people think about is the federal unemployment (UE) rate. This is the number reported by the BLS and shared throughout all the news outlets. The only issue with this published UE rate is that is not totally accurate. Let me explain how the UE rates are calculated.

There are actually 6 different unemployment rates: U1, U2, U3, U4, U5 and U6. The one that is commonly reported is the U3 unemployment rate. Simply put, this number is calculated by the BLS after contacting 60,000 random homes and surveying potential workers over the age of 16 who were available to work full-time in the past four weeks.   Plus, the surveyed potential workers must have actively been looking for work during the past four weeks.   However, anyone who does not meet this narrow definition of unemployed is not considered unemployed for the monthly published UE calculation.   So, the U3 formula looks like this:

Unemployment Rate = Unemployed / Civilian Labor Force

(Note: the Civilian Labor Force is defined as those employed and who meet the definition of unemployed as explained above.)

As I mentioned earlier, the U3 UE rate is not totally accurate because there are other groups of people who are not working. These groups include people who have looked for work in the past 12 months, just not in the past four weeks, and feel there is no work available for a specific reason (discouraged workers); people who are available to work, willing to work, not discouraged to look for work, but just did not look in the past four weeks; and people who work part-time because they cannot find full-time work due to economic conditions. So if you want a totally accurate unemployment rate, take the unemployed found in the U3 calculation, add in the three additional out-of-work groups, and the final number will be the total number of people who are not working - the more accurate U6 unemployment rate. Unfortunately, since you need to do more digging into the numbers to get the more accurate U6 UE rate, and since the U3 UE rate is what is commonly reported, I will use the U3 UE rate for our discussion on the labor market.

As of October, 2018, the federal UE rate was 3.7% - the lowest since 1969. The U6 rate for October was 7.4%. More importantly for our discussion on the labor market and skilled labor availability, this is the 25th consecutive month below 5%, and only once in the past 29 months did unemployment reach 5% (Sept. 2016). The unemployment rates for African-American and Hispanics are reaching all-time lows, as are the rates for teenagers, less-educated Americans and disabled.

Additionally, as more and more employers become global in nature, they have to compete against the global unemployment situation. So just to present a quick global comparison, during 2018, unemployment rates of other countries with skilled workforces also showed low unemployment: China at 3.9%, Germany at 3.6%, South Korea at 3.6%, Mexico at 3.4%, Switzerland at 3.2% and Japan at 2.4%.

The next number to look at is the labor force availability rate. This rate measures the number of employed and unemployed persons divided by the civilian population. Note: the civilian population is defined as the eligible workers, over the age of 16, both employed and unemployed, but, have searched for a job within the past four weeks, and are not incarcerated. Again, it is important to note, this number does not take into consideration those potential workers who have not searched for a job in the past four weeks. However, this number also does not take into consideration those potential workers who WANTED a job, but for some reason or another, couldn't search for a job.

The labor force availability rate for October 2018 was 62.9%. To look at this in a historical perspective, the labor force availability rate peaked in 2000 at 67.3%, but after two recent recessions (2001 and 2008), the rate has fallen and hoovered around the low 60% level since.

What the labor force availability rate means is roughly 37% of the civilian population was eligible to work but has elected NOT to participate in the workforce for some reason or another. The reasons why someone would give up working or looking for a job are health or disability, age, tired of looking and discouraged, or, unfortunately, a victim of the opioid crisis.

So looking at the numbers, with unemployment and the labor force availability rate so low, it is extremely challenging for recruiters to fill open vacancies. There just are not enough available skilled workers to fill existing vacancies, let alone any new jobs created by companies that are growing. If you do not believe me, just ask any recruiter and he/she will tell you how difficult it is to fill a vacancy. And to add salt to the wound so to speak, the federal government recently announced that there were more job openings (over seven million) than there are potential workers (under six million).

With such a shortage in the labor market, it is critical for an organization to continue to focus not only on recruiting the top talent it needs for current and future vacancies, but increase efforts on retaining the skilled labor the organization currently has in its workforce.

Chapter 7

So, What Is The Answer?

I know you have been waiting to find the "silver bullet" answer to keeping your skilled labor from applicant to retirement. However, I believe before you can be proactive and start to implement change, it was important to have the discussion about yourself as a leader, what the motivation factors are, what the current labor market data shows and how diverse the labor market is. It is difficult to move forward if you do not know where you are starting from. But before I share what is the answer, I think it is important to state what IS NOT the answer: to do nothing!

There is so much research out there on why people join an organization and then, over time, end up leaving before retirement. This phenomenon occurs because an organization stops changing as the workforce changes and becomes stagnant. (Remember: a company should focus on its greatest asset: its employees....the people who make the product or provide the service, who sell it, who service it, who collect payment for it, as well as the leaders who guide the organization.) So when an organization focuses on the RETENTION of its key performers, even its core group of workers, retention rates rise and the organization is able to keep its skilled talent where it belongs: inside the organization.

Beverly Kaye and Sharon Jordan-Evans wrote in their book, *Love 'em or Lose 'em* (Berrett-Koehler Publishers, Fifth edition), that there are 10 reasons why employees would stay with an organization:

1. Exciting work and challenge
2. Career growth, learning and development
3. Working with great people
4. Fair pay
5. Supportive management/good boss
6. Being recognized, valued and respected
7. Benefits
8. Meaningful work and making a difference
9. Pride in the organization, its mission and its products
10. Great work environment and culture

Ceridian did a global study and published in its *2017 Pulse of Talent Report* the five reasons high-performing employees stayed with an organization:

1. Good relations with colleagues
2. Good salary
3. Interesting work
4. Good working conditions
5. Job security

Andrew Chamberlain reported in the *Harvard Business Review* (March 6, 2017) the reasons why employees stayed:

1. Promotion and career progression
2. Competitive pay
3. Culture
4. Good working relationship with their manager

I think it would be safe to say employees would become active seekers and start looking for a new job because of the opposite of the reasons above. For example:

1. If you do not pay your employees competitively, at least in their local market, then they will start looking for a new job that meets their financial expectations.
2. If you do not have a culture where employees are recognized for doing good work or going above and beyond what is normally expected, they will go find an organization that will appreciate them.
3. If you do not promote those employees who have invested their hard work and efforts into the success of the organization, then they will go where an organization will recognize them for their efforts.
4. If you do not invest in the training and professional development of your employees, preventing them from becoming stagnant and "outdated" in their skills, then they will go to an organization that will invest in them, just as they have invested in the organization.
5. If you do not provide a career path, a future, for your employees – for as long as they want to work for the organization, then they may use your organization as a "stopover" on their journey to a fulfilling, life-long career.

Times have changed since I first entered the workforce over 40 years ago. Back then, diversity was still new and hardly discussed. Only two, may three, generations existed in the workplace. We were just starting to identify an organization's culture. Employees did as they were told and did not challenge their manager, nor ask the manager for the reasons why, they were being asked to do something. There were no expectations of the organization to invest and take care of the employees beyond what was legally required. You were paid what the organization wanted to pay, not what you expected nor even what the local market dictated. Promotions were generally based upon your tenure with the organization, not your achievements. And organizations did not have to worry about the Internet, social media or even cell phones being utilized by its employees at their workstations!

Today, the workplace environment is totally different. Diversity is not only discussed, but it focused upon from the very instant an applicant is exposed to the organization to the day the employee leaves the organization. We have up to 5 generations in the workplace. Employees have expectations when it comes to the organization being socially responsible, for their jobs and professional development, on promotions, competitive pay and benefits, a work/life balance, being able to use the Internet and their cell phones at their workstations – even while on the clock, on recognition/promotions and rewards, and being able to voice their opinions and seeing management putting their opinions into action. Yes....a lot has changed, at least for me, since the mid-70's!

So here I am, 40-plus years later. Hopefully, I am a tad wiser on this journey throughout my professional life. I can honestly say I have learned more than I ever thought I would have since I first entered the workplace. Luckily, I was in positions, as well as in occupations, that allowed me to work with others, at all levels of the organization, in different industries and in different parts of the country, that helped me grow to become the HR professional I am today. And the greatest aspect of the position

I am in now, as an educator and leader in the business community, is I can share what I have learned so that others just beginning their journey can benefit from this experience.

Okay….it is time! I would like to introduce my construct…my theory…my philosophy…my "silver bullet" so to speak, on how you can keep a person at your organization from applicant to retirement (assuming the person has the desire to stay that long, of course). It may seem quite simple, but just because it seems simple does not mean it is easy. It takes a commitment, with dedicated resources, and a culture that promotes and supports.

I believe there are five aspects in an employee's career that, if taken care of properly, will allow the employee to remain with the organization, satisfied and engaged, from the minute the orientation is over until retirement. The acronym for the five aspects is "P. A. P. E. R." and is spelled out as such:

1. P – Pay
2. A – Achievement
3. P – Promote
4. E – Educate
5. R – Retirement

The construct is this: if you take care of the employee's "P. A. P. E. R.", then you will have an employee from applicant to retirement. Now let us look at each aspect in greater detail.

Chapter 8

"P" – Pay

Ahhh....the almighty paycheck....the most basic link between the employee and the employer in the employment relationship! And being so basic, one would think it would be easy to set a fair wage that would be acceptable to an employee and ensure the employee's loyalty to the organization. Regrettably, it is not that basic.

The first issue to consider is the actual wage being offered. Is it "fair"? In the employee's perception, a fair wage is one that pays the bills, as well as compensates for the hard work performed. Using the motivational theories discussed in Chapter 5, under Maslow's theory, earning enough to pay the bills would be a physiological motivation, the bottom level of his pyramid. Under Herzberg's theory, paying the bills would be a hygiene factor; again, a basic motivational factor. As far as paying the employee what he/she would believe to be a fair wage for the hard work performed, this would be found under the expectancy theory because the employee has an expectation on what the value of his/her work is.

Now, the organization's perception of a fair wage is one that is both internally, within the organization – called internal equity, and externally, within the local, geographical job market in the organization is located – called external equity, competitive for the duties the employee is performing. Let me explain this concept by using an example.

I want to make sure the pay for a Customer Service Representative, CSR, is competitive. To start, I will look inside the organization and see where the CSR pay falls within the hierarchy of job titles within the organization? Then, I can do a quick Google search and see what the average pay range is for CSRs in the local job market. If the pay is competitive in the job market, then the pay will probably be fair. But I would suggest a third step. I will look at the turnover in the Customer Service Department. If I see there is a lot of turnover in the Department, I will check the exit interviews to see if the CSRs were leaving because of wages. If the reason was because of low wages, then I can see about making adjustments to the pay ranges for CSR within the organization.

(Note: most pay guidelines are determined by members of the HR team who specialize in compensation. These folks perform a job analysis to ensure the job descriptions and job duties are accurate for the job title. They then obtain market survey data to determine if the pay is competitive in the marketplace.)

Another influence on the issue of pay is the push for what is called a "living wage". This is a national movement supported by organized labor groups pushing for an increase of the federal minimum hourly wage to $10 an hour, with some groups pushing for as high as $15 an hour. However, this wage adjustment is not based upon an increase in the education, skills or training of the workers. The objective is to implement an automatic increase of minimum wage to establish a new "floor" from which wages are based upon.

What is minimum wage? The federal minimum wage, as regulated by the Fair Labor Standards Act (1938), is currently at

$7.25 per hour and equates to about $15,080 annualized. This is just a few thousand over what the federal government considers as the federal poverty level; thus, the push to raise minimum wage. However, per the BLS, the estimates are about only 700,000 workers, which include part-time workers, are being paid at the federal minimum wage. Most workers making a minimum wage are not making the federal minimum wage but are making their state's minimum wage because most states have a higher minimum wage and the state wage overrules the federal wage.

Sadly, the federal minimum wage has been $7.25 since 2009! That is almost nine years without an adjustment...and we all know that the price for EVERYTHING has gone up over the past nine years. Also, most states use the federal minimum wage as the base wage, the floor, to work from. Thus, when the federal minimum wage goes up, so does the state wage proportionately. But if the federal minimum wage does not go up, then the state minimum wage may not go up. (NOTE: federal contractors have a higher minimum wage set at $10.10 per hour per Executive Order.) Unfortunately, the costs for goods and services keep going up year over year and that is the argument to raise minimum wage: to keep up with rising costs.

A challenge with raising the federal minimum wage to a living wage, such as to $10 an hour all at once versus gradually over time, is where will the money for the increased employee hourly wages come from? Since wages are a part of the total cost of the goods or services the organization provides, the wage increases will be passed onto the consumer who is buying the goods or services. Thus, while you may be getting more money in your paycheck, you will be paying higher prices for the goods you buy because you have to help pay for the higher wages the workers are now earning.

A third issue to consider is what happens when state or local governments make their own adjustments to minimum wage? This may seem simple enough to address...unless your organization happens to be regional or national in nature and now you are forced to look at and address geographical wage differences. Oh.....and what if your organization has global operations? Now you have to consider the laws of the host country your organization is working in. Do I hear a "gasp" about now?????

In my local market, when the city my company is based in tried to raise the minimum wage (just inside the city limits) to $10.00 an hour, which was over $2.20 per hour higher than the state minimum wage, all sorts of negative actions took place. Businesses, large and small, threatened to move, and some did move, out of my city's limits because literally right across the street in the next city, minimum wage was still lower. Lobbying activities took over at the state level and our state government passed legislation preventing cities from implementing their own minimum wages. (Note: cities were allowed to set minimum wage requirements for city workers.)

Oh, before I forget. Many organizations have an employee policy that states employees cannot discuss their wages with other employees. If an employee is caught, the employee is subject to a disciplinary action or even termination. Is your company one of them? If so, BE CAREFUL! The folks at the National Labor Relations Board (NLRB) believe employees have a right to discuss their wages with fellow employees without fear of disciplinary action. To the NLRB, this is a protected concerted activity and is subject to regulatory action by the NLRB.

My final note on pay: PAY ASSOCIATES WITHOUT CONSIDERATION TO GENDER! I have been supporting fair and equal pay for all workers my entire career...well before any protests or organized movements. Why? Because it is very simple: it is HR's duty!!! HR must oversee pay decisions and if necessary, put the "blinders" on those who manage pay decisions when it comes to compensation. If an employee is qualified and trained, then the employee should be paid fairly and equally – regardless of gender, as well as race, color, creed, national origin, age, Veteran status, disability, pregnancy, sexual orientation or identity, or any other protective status.

Now that we are paying our employees properly, the next step to making sure our employees want to stay is to recognize them for their contributions to the organization.

Chapter 9

"A" – Achievement

There is a lot of research out there on the value of recognizing employees for the work they do. This value impacts the organization in many ways: contributes to an employee-focused culture, improves morale, allows employees to feel their work is valued, increases employee productivity, and most importantly, improves employee retention!

Some organizations prefer to focus only on the high performers and spend its limited resources on recognizing these high performers. However, high performers do not comprise the majority of the organization's workforce. Jack Welch, former Chief Executive Officer of General Electric, used to say organizations should focus on the top 20 percent of its workforce and do what it takes to retain these top performers. These top performers are your key employees...your rising stars. Then, he said to focus on the next 60 percent of the workers because they are your day-to-day workers who get the job done. (For the remaining 20 percent, he recommended assisting them look for a different job where they would be more successful). That is roughly 80 percent of the workforce that an organization needs to focus on in order to retain this skilled talent. So, how can an organization recognize its workers?

A good definition of recognition is the timely, informal or formal, acknowledgement of a person's or a team's behavior, effort or business result that supports the organization's goals and values, and which has clearly been beyond normal expectations. However, I want to make sure there is a clear distinction between recognizing employees for the work they do under a recognition program and recognizing employees under a merit program. (Note: I will discuss recognition under the performance review process in the next chapter as the performance review is frequently used when determining the upward mobility of an employee.)

Under a merit program, employees receive increases to their pay based upon the guidelines of a formal merit increase program. For example, at the end of a performance rating period, employees are given merit pay increases based upon the performance review rating they received.

Under a recognition program, employees receive recognition for exceeding expectation for completion of a one-time event or a special project. Normally, this recognition does not involve an increase in the employees' regular wages. For example, when a team of employees complete a special project and deserve to be recognized, they will receive recognition in the organization's e-newsletter, in front of their peers at the organization town hall meeting and a gift showing thanks for all the hard work performed.

Did you know, many employees do not feel appreciated for their work? This is a sorry statement to hear, especially for those of us in the HR community. However, the research supports this statement. In 2016, Gallup conducted a survey and found that only 1 in 3 US workers felt they received recognition or praise for doing good work in a seven day period. Follow the Gallup survey with surveys conducted by Sirota Consulting. Sirota Consulting administered surveys over a 10-year period, to over 2.5 million employees in 89 countries in private, non-profit and public organizations, and found that only 51% of the workers were satisfied with the recognition they received for their work. WOW! That means 49 percent of the workers did NOT feel they were being recognized. Think of that! Would you want to work somewhere where you are not appreciated and recognized for the hard work you do????

Another key component in recognizing an employee is to make sure when you do recognize an employee, either formally or informally, that the employee finds value in the recognition. The challenge with recognition programs is they are normally "one size fits all" programs. Unfortunately, our workforce is a diverse group and one size does not fit all. Remember the discussion in chapter 5 about intrinsic and extrinsic motivation? Employees are motivated either intrinsically or extrinsically....or maybe even both! For example, when I do something at work that is outside my normal job duties, and I exceed expectations, I find more value in intrinsic recognition, such as seeing my name up on the organization's message board, than receiving a monetary gift card. (Note: my wife will totally disagree...she would prefer the gift card!)

Recognition programs may range from informal, with little to no structure, to formal, with inflexible and rigid guidelines and processes in place. Both have their own merits, as well as challenges. To me, it seems organizations tend to go with the more formal programs. However, experts like Dr. Bob Nelson believe informal recognition is invaluable because informal recognition is normally inexpensive, if not free, and is much more timely than formal recognition. (Note: check out Bob Nelson's book, *"1501 ways to reward employees"*.) So, I think it is wise to look at both and, if possible, implement both at your place of employment. Let me share some examples of both informal and formal recognition programs.

Informal recognition is a simple as walking up to an employee who has exceeded expectations and thanking the employee, in front of his/her peers, for the accomplishment he/she achieved. So simple to do; cost: nothing! Another idea of informal recognition is to post an employee's achievement in a company newsletter or on a message board. Again, simple to do minimal cost!

Formal recognition, on the other hand, should be structured, have eligibility rules, defined rewards, a set timeframe to present the recognition to the deserving employee, etc., etc, etc. Again, the program is formal. For example, under formal recognition, when an employee goes above and beyond, the employee's action (positive behavior) is written up on a recognition nomination form, which is then forwarded to HR for processing. Usually, the nomination form requires approval. Once approved, the recognition award is identified. The cost of the award is usually based upon the perceived value, or amount of effort, of the positive behavior of the employee performed. (In some cases, you may want to personalize the award.) Next, the date to present the recognition to the employee is set. In many cases, the award presentation is delayed until the next formal company/department scheduled meeting. Finally, at the scheduled meeting, the employee receives official recognition. Wow....lots of steps....lots of delays....and there will be some costs involved!

An example of a formal recognition program is what I like to call an "Above and Beyond" program. This program is simple but, unfortunately, is also a "one size fits all" type program. Under this program, there are two award levels, Spot and Full, and is based upon what positive behavior the employee is being recognized for.

To receive Spot recognition, an employee does something that is a one-time event, such as helping out a fellow employee. A supervisor or fellow employee would nominate the employee and send the nomination form to HR for processing. For Spot awards, HR already has pre-approval to approve these nominations. Once HR processes the nomination and approves it, HR issues the recognition award to the supervisor for immediate awarding to the deserving employee. I like to use a $25 gift card. Then, at the next scheduled company/department meeting, the employee will be recognized again by having their name listed as a Spot Award recipient.

To receive Full recognition, an employee does something over a period of time, such as completing a special project that provides value to the organization, to the department or even to a customer. A nomination form is completed and processed by HR. An award is determined, purchased and prepared for presentation. However, unlike the Spot award, this award is presented at the next scheduled organization/department meeting so the organization president can make the presentation. For the Full award, I like to use a $50 to $100 gift card, plus a plaque and framed certificate of recognition.

Regardless if your recognition is under an informal or formal program, I think the key is the recognition to the employee must be timely. What I mean here is the time from the employee's achievement to the employee receiving recognition cannot be so long that the employee forgets what the recognition is for. Basically, you do not want to lose the "bang for the buck". Remember, recognition is rewarding the employee for doing something good – which is called a positive behavior. So, if you want the employee to continue the positive behavior, the supervisor or manager should reward timely so the employee will continue to perform in a positive manner. The recognition by the employee's supervisor or manager reinforces the positive behavior...that is the behavior you want from the employee. (Note: this is basic behavior modification and operant conditioning. For more information, start with B. F. Skinner.)

Recognizing employees is a key factor to retention. It is a key to improving employee morale and engagement. It is a key to the success of an organization. Dr. Lawrence Hrebiniak, Professor of Management in the Wharton School at the University of Pennsylvania, wrote that these positive employee behaviors must be recognized and reinforced. An organization must recognize the success of its employees. Dr. Hrebiniak believes by giving recognition and positive feedback, organizations will be successful. (Note: check out Dr. Hrebiniak's book: *"Making strategy work: leading effective execution and change".*)

Chapter 10

"P" – Promote

Promoting employees is critically beneficial to both the employee and the organization. Think about it. From the employee's perspective, the promotion represents an increase in responsibility, a new job title, praise from co-workers and an increase in wages. From the organization's viewpoint, the promotion means recognizing an employee for his/her performance and commitment to the organization, the opportunity to give the employee more responsibility in the organization's day-to-day operations and, hopefully, increases the retention and engagement of the promoted employee. Together, this "win-win" scenario will improve the morale within the organization because the organization is showing its commitment and loyalty to the workforce. Plus, the increase in employee engagement will result in higher productivity and in the end, higher profits earned by the organization.

Most employees, to include managers, believe promotions are easy to do. The organization determines who will be promoted, what the new rate of pay will be and when the effective date will be. Once implemented, everyone will be happy with the promotion. Sounds so easy...right???? WRONG! There are many obstacles and pitfalls to watch out for when dealing with promotions. But before you consider promoting someone or not, make sure you determine if the position that you have vacant is one that can be filled from within (through succession planning) or one that you will have to go outside the organization and hire off the street (with replacement hiring).

Most positions within an organization can be filled by someone currently working inside the organization. It is common to see an ambitious employee over time promote up from hourly worker to lead, to supervisor, then to manager and even to department leader. One organization I am familiar with, a multi-million dollar organization with over 200 employees, has an individual who first started working in the warehouse as a supervisor and after 25 years, is now the president!

Succession planning is where organizations identify potential employees who possess the knowledge, skills and ability (KSA), or they have demonstrated the aptitude to gain additional knowledge and learn new skills, and place the employees in development plans to prepare them for the next level up. Think of a major league baseball team. Every major league baseball team has teams in the minor leagues where players are drafted and then developed and groomed for potential promotion to the next level of play (such as from A to AA, or AA to AAA); ultimately reaching the major league level if the player has the KSA to be successful. The same idea applies within organizations: the organization identifies and creates professional development plans to help guide the employee as the employee grows within the organization. (NOTE: This advancement over the years, within the same organization, must have senior leadership oversight, be managed by the HR Department and have the training and development support for each role in order to properly develop the employee for success in the next role.) When done correctly, succession planning is less expensive when compared to hiring qualified applicants from outside the organization.

WARNING: an organization never should promote just for the sake of promoting or to try and retain someone who is not qualified for the next level. When an organization promotes an unprepared employee, the organization runs the risk of "promoting for failure" and this could not only lead to lower productivity, poor morale and less employee engagement, it could result in the employee to leave the organization and take all his/her experience and knowledge away from the organization.

If, on the other hand, the organization determines that a vacancy cannot be filled internally, then the organization must go outside and hire someone off the street who already possesses the KSAs needed for the vacancy. This is called replacement hiring. For example, in my current role, there is no one inside my organization who can take my job if I leave. So, when my time comes, the organization will need to recruit from the outside a skilled HR Generalist, with labor experience, to take my place. The company could do the recruiting in-house (to save on recruiting costs) or secure the services of a headhunter/recruiting firm (and pay the finder's fee). Keep in mind studies show when you hire off the street at "current market wages", it is more expensive than if an organization promotes from within.

Okay, so you have decided you can promote from within. But how do you make sure you are implementing and following a viable promotion process at work? Let us look at some of the challenges to a promotion process and how you can avoid making a promotion a negative event at work versus a positive event for all.

The first consideration in creating a viable promotion process is to remember the government has laws and regulations that could impact your promotion process. For example, an employer cannot discriminate against an employee in any way, to include training opportunities and promotions. Without going into all the laws, regulations, rules and guidance letters, you should start with the Uniform Guidelines on Employee Selection Procedures. (http://www.uniformguidelines.com) These guidelines take into consideration the federal laws, regulations and rules that prevent any form of discrimination in all aspects of the employment relationship, from applicant to retirement, to include promotions. Also, you want to make sure your promotion process conforms to the Uniformed Services Employment and Reemployment Rights Act for your employees who are in the US [military] National Guard or Reserves. (https://www.dol.gov/vets/programs/userra) (NOTE: once you are familiar with the federal laws that impact a promotion process, make sure you do not have state and local laws that could potentially impact your promotion process as well.)

The next challenge you face is how to determine who is and is not promotable. I mentioned in the last chapter we would discuss performance reviews here because most of us use the performance management review process to obtain data to determine who the potential promotable employees are.

The performance review is a dual-edged sword in my opinion. When done correctly, it provides accurate information about an employee, as well as helps plan out the future development options for the employee. However, when done incorrectly, it could not only document inaccurate performance data about an employee, it could also demotivate an employee to the point the employee totally disengages from the organization and the employee initiates a job search for a new organization to work for.

Simply stated, when you complete a performance review, performance data is obtained from some form of feedback or measurement device: financial analytics, job performance evaluation metrics or comments from others who interact with the person being rated. Some of the performance data is objective in nature, is difficult to corrupt or manipulate, and is obtained from other automated software/measuring devices feeding into the review process. For example, if one of your objectives on your performance review is to make $100,000 in top line sales, and you reached $120,000 per your accounting software, then you accurately exceeded your goal and this will be inserted into your performance review for that particular objective.

Unfortunately, most feedback in the traditional performance review is subjective in nature; thus, the opportunity for inaccurate data - also called contamination error. Three of the most common examples of this contamination are:

1. rater error: where a rater evaluates too easy or too hard as compared to other raters
2. recency effect: where the rater only evaluates based upon the most recent events before the performance review is completed
3. halo/horn effect: where the rater assumes the person being rated is always a great worker (halo) or always a bad worker (horn)

The key to a successful performance review is to make sure the review accurately reflects the performance of the individual for the entire review period, not just a portion of the review period. Additionally, remember a performance review is NOT a disciplinary document. If an individual's performance is poor and action is needed to get the performance to improve, don't wait until it is time to complete the performance review. Initiate a corrective action plan as soon as the undesirable behavior is discovered.

Here is a tool, a very inexpensive by the way; you can use to identify potential promotable employees. I call it the "Post It" assessment and it works like this. The next time a talent evaluation is to be conducted, gather the evaluators into a room and hand each a stack of Post It notes. Ask each evaluator to write down the name, one name per Post It, of the individuals to be evaluated. While the evaluators are writing down the names, go to a wall and after visually splitting the wall horizontally in half, tape up a horizontal line about two inches in height (can easily be made out of different colored Post It notes or use white copy paper). You should now have a "display" on the wall with space above and below the horizontal line. Next, on the left end of the "display" and above the line, tape up a sign that says "Promotable" and under the line tape up a sign that reads "Not Promotable Today". Now that the "display" is created, ask each evaluator to take his/her stack of Post It notes with the names on them and place each individual Post It note where they believe the evaluated individual (whose name is on the Post It) should be on the "display" - above the line or below. Once the "display" is full of names, the discussion can begin about the evaluated employees. For example, one evaluator may have information about an evaluated employee that another evaluator may not and this may move the evaluated employee up or below the line.

Other factors that can be used in the decision to promote an employee could be the length of service (tenure) with the organization, education/technical qualifications or experience as a lead or supervisor.

My final thought on promotions has to deal with the actual promotion process itself; in particular, how the employees feel about the promotion process. There are two key questions to ask about any systemic process: is the process built to do what it supposed to do and does the process produce the results accurately?

The first question deals with a concept called procedural justice. Here employees must feel the promotion process is designed correctly to collect and examine all the relevant information necessary to make the promotion decision. For example, was the internal job vacancy posted in all areas for all employees to see? Another example would be when evaluating internal applicants, were all internal applicants, who expressed an interest in the opening, given the chance to interview with the decision makers, even if it was just a courtesy interview, or were they denied an interview all together?

The second question deals with a concept called distributive justice. Here employees must feel the promotion process provides accurate results; meaning, the person who received the promotion was justified in that promotion. The worst violation of distributive justice is when the applicant chosen, who went through the promotion process and was determined to have lower assessment scores than the other internal applicants, was promoted solely on the basis he/she was a friend or relative of the decision maker. (Think "good ole boy" club or even worse, nepotism!)

Remember, when dealing with internal promotions, all the candidates are known by someone else in the organization. There are perceptions, accurate or inaccurate, about the candidates. Even when the promotion process is working (procedural justice is working), if the outcome is perceived to be in error and the wrong person is selected (distributive justice is not working), then the next time an internal promotion opportunity arises, internal candidates may be apprehensive, or even resistant, to apply for the opening. And when this occurs, your opportunity to groom and grow your future leaders is in serious jeopardy!!!

Chapter 11

"E" – Educate

I found a quote on the Internet recently about educating our employees. The quote is, "The only thing worse than training your employees and having them leave is not training them and having them stay!" Some credit Henry Ford, founder of Ford Motor Company, with the saying, but regardless of who said it first, I think that quote is as accurate today as it was a hundred years ago. Think about it. Why would you want to keep employees who are no longer current on technology or practices in your industry? Would that not that hurt your business?

Let me put it into simple business terms: to run a business, you must invest! For example, you have to invest capital to purchase adequate space, raw materials/inventory, modern equipment and up-to-date software and technology. This investment in key assets is critical to sustain and grow your business. However, when I read an organization's website, it usually reads that "our employees are our greatest asset"! So, would it not seem logical that you would want to invest in your "greatest asset" – your employees? Are not your employees your greatest differentiators from your competition? (Note: Millennials expect educational opportunities to be a part of their professional development while working in an organization.)

Plus, and it should come as no surprise, it is cheaper to focus on the employees you currently have on staff and train them up versus going out into a tight labor market and trying to recruit the skilled talent you need. And take a quick look at the benefits the organization gains by committing to its investment in training the workforce: improved retention, improved job satisfaction and engagement, improved loyalty, improved productivity and even improved recruiting efforts. But before you can focus on your current employees, you need to make sure you have an understanding of what your organization needs as far as knowledge, skills and abilities (KSAs).

An easy process to determine what KSAs are needed is the skills needs analysis. To perform the skills needs analysis, you first identify the essential skills needed for your critical positions within the organization. Next, you need to look at the employees occupying those positions and see what skills they possess – for both today and in the future. Then you do a gap analysis to determine if the current employees possess those essential skills needed. If they do, great! If not, then you have a gap that needs to be filled by either training up the current employees (upskill training) or by going out to the labor market and hiring for those skills (right skill hiring).

Need another reason to invest in your employees? Look at more research!

A recent survey shows that 40 percent of the employees who receive poor training in their first year of employment will leave. Another survey stated that 65 percent of millennial workers believe it is the organization's responsibility to provide professional development while on the job.

Workforce 2030: A Call to Action, a report co-authored by Ted Abernathy and Greg Payne, reported the Baby Boomer generation is retiring at the alarming rate of 10,000 every day! Plus, many of those retiring are from the skilled trades, where 53 percent of skilled trade workers are over the age of 45. So the question becomes how are you going to replace the skilled talent loss?

Another area to look at is the cost of turnover: it is expensive! One outplacement organization states that the cost to replace a skilled worker can be anywhere from 20% to 200% of the annual wage for the lost worker, depending upon the job title and duties performed. The Society of Human Resource Management (SHRM) estimates the cost to lose a salaried employee making $40,000 a year would be between 6 to 9 months' salary on average. Wow...that is $20,000 to $30,000 in expenses to cover the recruiting and training costs, lost productivity and the indirect cost of the extra work added to other workers.

Also, look into your crystal ball and see what will be the future business trends, what new skills will be needed to compete and grow in your industry, and what will be needed to just keep pace with an ever-changing workplace? The World Economic Forum projects that by 2030, 65 percent of the workforce will be in jobs that did not exist in 2018!

Seems to me to be pretty easy to argue the need – no, the necessity – for organizations to look internally and heavily invest in the current workforce to train and prepare the workforce for the future. And research conducted by TrainingMag.com shows US businesses spent over $70 billion in 2016 on direct employee training initiatives alone. These billions do not even reflect the indirect costs, such as lost productivity, associated with taking employees away from their workstations and placing them in training programs.

So, how do we educate and train our workers? Well, there are several ways an organization can do this. For example, if you need certification in a specific technical or computer skill, you could send your employees to an organization that specializes in that training, a technical college or maybe even the community college. (Note: this type of training is normally found under an organization's professional development program.) On the other hand, if you need specialized knowledge that comes from a college degree program, then you would fund the employees to attend a local college. (Note: this type of training in normally found under an organization's tuition reimbursement program.)

To help ensure you develop a viable training program, you need to consider factors such as:

1. What topic(s) are to be trained?
2. Who is to be trained?
3. How much money is committed to the training?
4. Will the training be done onsite or remotely?
5. Will the training be hands-on or virtual?
6. How much time will be allocated to get the training completed?
7. Will the training be created in-house, bought off the shelf or tailored to your specific need?
8. Will the training be facilitated by a qualified in-house trainer or an outside trainer?
9. Who will do observations to ensure the training is actually being performed by the attendees once they complete the training?

A key to a viable training program is to have senior leadership support. Not only is this needed to secure the required dollars and training materials for the program, but without leadership support, training will not be a priority.

Another key to a viable training program is to ensure you are getting a good return on the investment (ROI) on the time, expense, resources and time away from the workstation dedicated to the training. More importantly, the ROI is a critical component in getting senior leadership to commit to the training. Granted, the ROI is important, but it is not the most critical factor with employee training. The goal with employee training is to make sure the new training is being implemented and sustained by the trained employee back at his/her workstation.

So, how do you determine what the ROI is? What metric, or metrics, will you need to validate the training is being performed back at the workstations? Needless to say, this is not the easiest task to undertake because many times, when conducting training, the trainer is trying to change behaviors of the trainees. The trainer wants the trainees to do specific tasks a new or different way from the current way of doing things; but changing behavior takes time. (NOTE: for more on changing behavior, read up on the Organizational Behavior Modification Model. This model has been shown to improve performance and productivity much higher than our typical performance review process.)

There are plenty of books on the market that discuss the ROI from effective training. Don't believe me? Just Google or surf Amazon.com. For the purposes of this book, I would like to simplify the process and share a checklist to evaluate your training program. This checklist was developed by Michael Scriven is easy to use. Scriven's 12-point Training Evaluation Checklist (TEC) is an instrument to help develop a training program, as well as evaluating the training program to see if it is doing what it was intended to do. The TEC may be modified for smaller, less costly training programs or expanded to deeply evaluate elaborate, high cost training programs. The only difference is in the depth of the questioning under each of the 12 checkpoints. But the key is that each checkpoint should be discussed.

The 12-point training evaluation checklist is:

1. Need
2. Design
3. Recruitment
4. Delivery
5. Reaction
6. Learning
7. Retention
8. Application
9. Extension (or Generalizability)
10. Value
11. Alternatives
12. Return on Investment (quantitative and qualitative)

Of course there is a lot more involved with Scriven's TEC, but I wanted to give you an idea on what you need to do to create a viable training program that will bring value to your employees. Again, looking at the numbers discussed earlier in this chapter, if we do not provide viable, usable training to our employees, where they perceive the training to be valuable to their careers, then our employees will go find an organization that will.

Chapter 12

"R" – Retirement

Remember the old saying, "there are two things guaranteed in life: death and taxes!" Well, recently I heard a radio commercial on the air that stated there are now three things we can look forward to in life: death, taxes and retirement! The radio ad was about retirement planning and how you are going to fund retirement. But when you think about the radio ad, it is true! Retirement IS something that, inevitably, every one of us will have to address as we get closer to the end of our work careers because, someday, our work life journey will come to an end.

As an organization, though, do you want the majority of your employees to stay until retirement? To answer that question, you need to have a good understanding of your organization in order to determine if keeping the majority of your employees until retirement is the right decision. You need to know the pros and cons to keeping employees all the way to retirement. For example, as the tenure of employees goes up, so does the cost for those employees. Can you afford keeping employees all the way to retirement? To help with this discussion, let us look at some of the pros and cons of keeping employees all the way to retirement.

Research has shown that there may be some detractors for long-tenured employees. For example, the longer you stay at one organization, the more "comfortable" you get. You like to keep doing things the same way (I call this the "DITWLY" disease: "did it that way last year"); you resist change –

especially in processes, procedures and technology; your new ideas, innovation, creativity and production may decline; your skills may become outdated; you and your other long-term employees engage in groupthink; or you may become resistant to embracing new hires and younger workers into your established group of coworkers.

Looking at the cost of tenured employees, they are more expensive! Employee wages will be higher, utilization of benefits – especially medical benefits – is higher (which results in higher health care premiums for all employees), pension and/or retirement benefits cost more and need to be accrued, more vacation time earned, etc….the list can go on and on. Is your organization financially ready for tenured employees to stay until retirement?

Another area to look at is the demographics or composition of your workforce. What does your workforce look like? Is your workforce mostly comprised of the same gender, same national origin, same color, same sexual orientation and same generation? Is it missing the inclusion of disabled – visible or invisible – or other protected classes? In other words, is everyone basically the same, leading to a homogenous workforce, where everyone thinks the same, acts the same and shares the same ideas? Regrettably, this leads to group think, with little to no introduction of new ideas or concepts, and a dysfunctional ability to respond to the changes that are occurring in the work environment on an ever-changing basis.

Taking it a step further, and actually a more important consideration for any business to address, you should consider what your customer base looks like? Is it homogenous like your workforce or is it a diverse community comprised of people of all ages, backgrounds, beliefs and customs, religions, physical abilities and personal needs and goals? As your organization focuses on providing the services and products for your diverse customer base, shouldn't your workforce mirror your customer base?

You are probably already aware of this, but the federal government, as well as many state and local governments, are more and more focused on diversity and inclusion in the workplace, today, than ever before and have established guidelines to improve diversity and inclusion. For example, the federal focus is coming from multiple departments, from different agencies, making it even more challenging. The agencies/departments are the Department of Labor, to include the EEOC and OFCCP, IRS and OSHA just to name a few. But regardless if the government is focused on your organization or not, it is good citizenship behavior and socially responsible for the organization to be demographically representative INSIDE the organization and resemble the demographics of the community it serves.

Whew! Sure seems like there are a lot of negatives to keeping employees until retirement. Thankfully, there are plenty of positives to keeping employees until retirement. For example, think about how much money is saved in recruiting costs, both direct and indirect, not to mention the costs to train new hires, by not having a lot of turnover. And when there are new hires, tenured workers make great mentors to aid in the learning curve of the new hires.

Tenured employees have a higher level of productivity and organizational knowledge, making them easy to cross-train on new areas within the organization or become members of work groups to address critical issues facing the organization. A lot of this knowledge comes from "on the job" experience versus what is learned in the classroom. Plus, as organizations go through changes over the years, tenured employees utilize their knowledge and experiences to navigate and adjust to the changes. Because they are skilled in their jobs, they can provide solutions to new problems, ideas for new growth and even be a vital part of the strategic planning process.

Tenured employees are also loyal employees, committed to the purpose of the organization and for the survival of the organization, especially during tough economic times or major changes. They reflect a stable work environment at the organization, which improves recruiting and retention. They become the defenders of an organization's culture and its history. With their knowledge of the past, they can help minimize the uncertainty of the future when decisions are made.

As you can see, there are pros and cons to having tenured employees who stay with the company until retirement. However, I believe the negatives to having tenured employees stay until retirement are far outweighed by the positives. But the ultimate decision to retain tenured employees until retirement must be made by the organization and will be based upon the purpose of the organization, the industry it is in, the local market, the economy, etc.

For an organization, the key to talent management is to have a good balance between long-tenured employees and those employees who have not been in the organization as long. Successful organizations that survive decade after decade are those with a culture that supports its long-tenured workforce, while at the same time offering a culture that welcomes new hires, people from all different backgrounds and beliefs, where everyone is committed to the mission and objectives of the organization.

Chapter 13

"P. A. P. E. R." – Does – "W. O. R. K."!

Now that you have discovered the secret of "P. A. P. E. R.", what do you do next? Well that is an easy question to answer. The next step is to put "P. A. P. E. R." into action! Make "P. A. P. E. R." - "W. O. R. K." for you!

What does "W. O. R. K." mean? Well, let me tell you. You now know when you take care of each component of "P. A. P. E. R." for your employees, the end result will be you will have long-term employees working for you. But what you may not realize is the lasting contribution of long-term employees to the company is their "W. O. R. K."! Let me explain.

Think about the benefits of having employees work for you year after year after year. What do you get in return? The obvious return is you have employees who know how to perform the job they are assigned to because they have so much time invested in performing those duties. They are skilled. They perform. They are masters of their craft. They take pride in their work because the results of their work represent them. This quality is called workmanship. (Workmanship – the "W")

Over the course of their career, long-term employees find ways to change with the times to ensure they remain at the top of their game. They learn how to operate new equipment. They learn about the new products and services being offered. They take the responsibility to make sure they do not become obsolete in their jobs. They become the mentors, the coaches, the "go to" people in a crisis. They provide the necessary feedback to leadership to remove obstacles, suggest improvements and develop new ideas to grow the organization. They help sustain the continuity within the organization as the organization grows over the years. The pride they have in their work permeates throughout the organization. Soon, others pick up on this sense of pride and begin to make sure they, too, are staying current with the changing times. (Openness – the "O")

The long-term employees also know that the consumer of their work, their customer, has high expectations and if these expectations are not met, then the consumer will go somewhere else to purchase what they need. We all know the marketplace, in any industry, is very competitive. So if the consumer decides to go somewhere else, then the organization would suffer in lost sales – which equates to lost revenue. Decreased revenue could (and probably will) negatively impact the employees of the organization through decreased wages or benefits, delays in improvements and modernization or even worse, job losses. Thus, to prevent this negative spiral from occurring, the organization and its employees need to work together to ensure the organization remains competitive. The organization has to invest in the workforce, ensuring up-to-date equipment is available and the workers are trained on current technology. This proactive responsibility by the employer to the employees, as well as the customer-focused responsibility by the employees to their customers, will not only help recruit the best talent, develop loyalty within a committed workforce and improve the retention of this highly skilled workforce, but will increase the loyalty from the customer base and improve customer retention. (Responsible – the "R")

Long-term employees know so much about the organization, such as the purpose and mission of the organization, who the customers are and how to take care of them, how the internal processes and procedures work, or who to go to when something needs to be fixed or get done quickly. Long-term employees know the history and trends of the organization. They have seen the ups and downs, been through the good and the bad. But more importantly, long-term employees know the culture of the organization. As a matter of fact, long-term employees are the DNA of the organization's culture. (I will discuss more about culture in the next chapter!) (Knowledgeable – the "K")

Maybe it is best to give you a real life example of "P. A. P. E. R." to show you how it works. To do so, let me introduce you to Steve.

Steve started working at a five year old warehousing company when he was in high school. His job was to clean the offices and work areas. He worked part-time during school and full-time during the holidays and summer. Steve used to joke how the owners would "lock him in the building" when they went to dinner so he would be safe while he worked. The years passed, then the decades; culminating forty-nine years later when Steve would retire from that same company.

At his retirement celebration, I had a chance to talk to Steve about what it was like to work for one company for so long. What was it that kept him there? Did he ever think about leaving? What motivated him to come to work every day, year in and year out? What did the company give him that he felt no other company could offer?

Steve had no hesitation in telling me that the reason why he stayed was because he believed in the company and the company believed in him. He said he was "old school", meaning he expected a good wage for a hard day's work. And that is what Steve did: he worked hard and devoted himself to the job he was assigned. In return, Steve believed he received a good wage to support himself and ultimately, his family. (This is the "P" for pay.)

Throughout his career, Steve learned new skills. He attended countless training courses, both for personal and professional development. (This is the "E" for educate.) This investment by the company in Steve paid off because in time, he became a recognized expert in his field. Additionally, over the span of his career, Steve was recognized for his professionalism, loyalty and performance to the company and promoted upward, leading four of the six departments at one time or another. (This is the "P" for promote.) There was even a time during a leadership transition when Steve led the entire company. Then upon his retirement, Steve was nationally recognized for his lifetime achievements to his profession. (This is the ultimate "A" for achievement.)

I asked Steve what he thought about when he reflected upon his career at this one company. He told me the company provided him what he wanted in a career: challenge, responsibility, opportunity to advance, a good income to raise his family and support his plans for retirement, and most of all, a good environment where people were committed to the job and to each other. The company provided him everything he wanted in a work career. (This is the "R" for retirement.)

Steve was truly thankful to the company for providing him a place to call his "second home" for over 49 years. And the company was just as thankful because Steve's contributions helped to turn a $100,000 start-up company (funny thing, the term "start-up" was not even used back in the mid-1960's) into the multi-million dollar organization it is today.

The company took care of Steve's "P. A. P. E. R" and Steve took care of the company through his "W. O. R. K.".

Chapter 14

Create a Great Culture!

Management guru Peter Drucker is given credit for saying, "Culture eats strategy for breakfast." What I interpret this to mean is an organization may establish great strategies to reach its objectives, but without a solid, positive culture in place within the organization, obtaining these strategies would be difficult to almost impossible. An organization's culture should cause others in the industry to change and imitate your organization. Why? It is because an organization's culture IS the organization! And the employees of the organization are the most important component of the organization's culture. Herb Kelleher, the former Chairman and CEO of Southwest Airlines once said, "The business of business is people; today, tomorrow and forever". Therefore, since this book is about the people in the organization, any discussion on recruiting and retaining top talent would not be complete without a discussion about culture!

Let us start the discussion with a definition of culture. An organization's culture is the shared values, attitudes and beliefs that describe the employees of the organization, as well as defines the focus of the organization. The culture is deeply engrained within the organization and is reflected in the organization's mission and vision, its goals and objectives, and how the organization treats its employees and the outlying community.

A key aspect of culture is it is always evolving, always changing; it is not static. In the beginning of the life cycle of an organization, the initial culture is established by the founder. The workforce is small, where everyone takes part, even assuming multiple roles beyond their official job description, in establishing the organization. The founder, or initial influencer, finds it easy to form and mold the culture of the organization. If changes are needed, the charisma of the founder makes it easy to implement the changes because the workforce trusts the founder.

As time goes on, the organization grows in size, adding layers of leadership, with increases in employees, customers and the influence the organization has on the community. Unfortunately, this growth brings challenges to sustain the organization's culture. For example, as the workforce grows, roles and responsibilities of the workforce become more specialized and compartmentalized. Thus, where once an employee felt connected to all areas of the organization, now the employee only feels connected to the department assigned, performing the duties assigned.

Additionally, the initial influencers of the organization's culture will find it more and more difficult to change the dynamics of the culture because there are now more layers within the organization and more stakeholders (employees, customers and the community) to convince to accept the change. It requires strong leadership to make changes to an established culture. To be successful, if the organization's leadership wants to make changes to the culture, they will need to get the employee base to agree to the changes. Remember, the culture should represent the shared values, attitudes and beliefs by all employees. Therefore, those who are committed to support the overall mission, goals and objectives of the organization must be convinced to make changes. If the culture is not shared, then dysfunction will set in because some employees will accept the change and other will resist the change.

So, how can you successfully influence the culture where you work? Look at these six easy steps.

The first step, and I think this is the easiest step, is to "walk the talk"! It is a fact: only YOU can control how you act. Thus, if your culture promote fairness, equality, honesty, open communication, transparency, procedural and distributive justice in decisions made, as well as following the laws of the land, then set the expectation – and enforce – for ALL employees to act this way. If you are a leader, LEAD by example! If you are a line worker, PERFORM by example. "Walk the talk" of the culture of your organization.

Second, when employees "walk the talk" and display positive behaviors that support the organization's culture, reward that behavior. Recognizing these positive behaviors reinforces the behaviors and makes them more permanent. Plus, when you recognize those displaying the positive behaviors, the workers who have not quite yet accepted the culture of the organization will observe the recognition and be more willing to "walk the talk".

Third, show empathy and respect for your employees. (Remember the term emotional intelligence and what it means?) When you show you care about your employees and will "go to bat" for them in difficult times, your employees will respond in kind. They know you have their best interest in mind when you make decisions. Thus, when you ask your employees to accept change, they will trust you and go with the change.

Fourth, when you "walk the talk", make sure you get out and "walk with the masses". This means get out of your work area and walk about the organization. Get to know the employee base and let them get to know you. Remove the invisible barriers or layers within the organization by visiting with everyone. This is called networking within the culture.

Fifth, when you are recruiting for new hires, discuss your culture and why it makes your organization so special. Make sure your interview questions discover if the applicant will fit into your culture. By doing so, not only do you make sure the applicant will be successful in the new position, but you make sure the applicant will integrate into your culture and support it. If you do not ensure the new hire will support your culture, you run the risk of hiring an applicant who could turn into a potential "cancer", one who could negatively impact your culture and slowly eat away at the culture you spent so much time developing and nurturing.

And finally, and this may be the hardest step, you need to have honest, open, straightforward, two-way dialogue with your employees. The message you communicate must be clear and easy to understand, avoiding confusing or incomplete information. Failure to provide a clear message could result in disinformation being shared throughout the organization, the spreading of inaccurate gossip, wrong actions taken, confusion, fear and even mistrust of the leaders making the decisions. Once you have established the communication channels, in times when the message is negative in nature, because the employees know and trust the person sending the message, they will accept and follow. This goes for the CEO of the organization, through the ranks of the leadership and management teams, all the way down to the line workers.

Seems like a lot of work to establish and sustain a positive culture. And do not forget, working on your culture will be in addition to your normal duties you were hired to do. But trust me on this: the commitment and effort are worth it!

Once you have a culture identified and in place, you will discover the employee engagement of your employees will elevate. Denison Consulting, LLC, researched and found that high employee engagement is an outcome of a healthy, positive culture. Denison also discovered the highest correlated item in their research between engagement and culture was when leaders and managers practiced what they preached.

Additionally, you will find recruiting and retention efforts will be easier because applicants/employees like to be associated with a successful, positive and supportive organization A friend of mine, who worked at one of the largest employers in my home town, told me when his organization was recognized as the "Best Places In America To Work For", the following year they received over three hundred thousand (yes, that is 300,000!!!!) unsolicited resumes!!! People want to work for a successful organization where the employee base is happy to work at that organization and proud to represent the organization to their family and friends in the community.

In this time of very low unemployment and small applicant pools of qualified workers, what would you rather have:

applicants searching for your organization and applying...or...having to spend your time and limited resources looking for applicants?

Use your culture to attract talented workers to your organization. Promote your organization and its positive culture in the community in which you reside. And use your culture to embrace and retain the skilled talent that makes your organization great for as long as they want to stay!

Chapter 15

Let's Wrap It All Up!

Well, there you have it. You have what I have been working on in my head for the past 30 plus years. You now know the secret of "P. A. P. E. R."!!!

I know I used a lot of numbers and research throughout the book to validate my viewpoints and conclusions, and I am sure some of the data will become outdated over time. However, the key concepts presented will not become outdated and will remain valid. This I am sure about.

We looked at many aspects associated with running a business, to include the impact of government rules and regulations, the U. S. economy and the composition of the labor market. There seems to be so many uncontrollable variables that are out of the control of the organization's leadership. Fortunately, government intervention, the availability of skilled talent in labor market or the economy in general, they all have cycles. For example, during the last recession (2008 – 2010), the U. S. economy was struggling, government regulations were considered heavily intrusive into the day-to-day operations of the private business sector, and the labor market was flooded with skilled talent as organizations cut headcount to control expenses. But today (2018), the U. S. economy is strong, government regulations have been modified, removed or returned to the wording found before the recession, and employers are growing and adding headcount as new jobs are created.

What this book attempts to accomplish, and I hope it exceeds your expectations, is to present a solid argument on why it is important to invest in yourself, as well as your workforce, to ensure the success of your organization. But more importantly, I hope I was able to provide you with some easy, simple, "tool kit" ideas that you can use to make your professional duties easier.

For those of you in the Human Resources profession, times are changing! We are becoming more and more of a strategic partner with an organization's leadership team because leadership understands the critical importance of talent management within their organization. Be the champions for your employees, the magnet for bringing in qualified applicants, the beacon for equality and justice and the moral compass for your organization. "Walk the Talk"!!!!! Not only will your leadership team acknowledge your commitment to the organization, your employee base will trust you and not hesitate to come to you in a time of need.

One last piece of free advice.....never...and I mean NEVER....stop being a life-long learner. Attend the free legal seminars offered in your community by local law offices. Take a college-level HR class. Get involved in community associations that focus on HR topics such as diversity and *inclusion*, those with disabilities, veteran integration back into the civilian sector, as well as your local HR association. Get a professional HR certification. Sign up for free email alerts on changes to government laws, rules and regulations.

For me, the next step in my journey is to conduct my own research to validate the "P. A. P. E. R." construct on an academic level. I plan to solicit HR professionals at organizations around the country to see if they, too, have long-term employees who have stayed with their organization from applicant to retirement. For those who respond affirmatively, I will survey those long-term employees for their feedback on why they stayed for an entire career. It is my hope the research will present the same type of feedback I received from Steve, the gentleman who retired at his company after 49 years and validate the theory of "P. A. P. E. R."!!!

"P. A. P. E. R." is a process, a philosophy and potentially a major shift in your culture….but, if you believe in what "P. A. P. E. R." stands for and follow it, then I am confident, over time, you will have a skilled and tenured workforce that will make your organization more competitive, retain the skilled talent you currently have and become the organization that future employees will want to come work for. And remember, if you utilize "P. A. P. E. R.", your workforce will "W. O. R. K." for you!!!!!!

28117213R00052

Made in the USA
Lexington, KY
13 January 2019